# ECOLOGY WA

# RAINFORESTS

## Rodn

DIL
N

First American publication 1991 by Dillon Press, Macmillan Publishing Company, 866 Third Avenue, New York, NY 10022

Macmillan Publishing Company is part of the Maxwell Communication Group of Companies

First published by Evans Brothers Limited, 2A Portman Mansions, Chiltern Street, London W1M 1LE.

Typeset by Fleetlines Typesetters, Southend-on-Sea
Printed in Spain by GRAFO, S.A. – Bilbao

**Library of Congress Cataloging-in-Publication Data**

Aldis, Rodney.
    Rainforests / by Rodney Aldis. – 1st ed.
      p. cm. – (Ecology watch)
    Includes index.
    Summary: Examines the plant and animal life of the rainforests and the threats to their continued existence.
    ISBN 0-87518-495-2
    1. Rain forest ecology – Juvenile literature. 2. Rain forests – Juvenile literature. 3. Rain forest conservation – Juvenile literature. [1. Rain forests. 2. Rain forest ecology 3. Ecology.] I. Title.
QH541.5.R27A43 1991
574.5'2642—dc20
                  91–20595

# Acknowledgments

**Editor: Su Swallow**
**Design: Neil Sayer**
**Production: Jenny Mulvanny**

Illustrations: David Gardner, Graeme Chambers
Maps and diagrams: Hardlines, Charlbury

For permission to reproduce copyright material the author and publishers gratefully acknowledge the following:

**Cover** Sally Morgan/ECOSCENE
**Title page** (eyelash viper) Michael Fogden, Oxford Scientific Films
**p4** Dr Morley Read, Science Photo Library **p5** (top) Michael Fogden, Oxford Scientific Films, (bottom) Alain Compost, Bruce Coleman Limited **p7** Wardene Weisser, Ardea London Ltd, (inset) M P L Fogden, Bruce Coleman Limited **p8** Dr Morley Read, Science Photo Library **p9** ECOSCENE **p10** Paul Franklin, Oxford Scientific Films **p11** Mark Edwards, Still Pictures **p12** Alain Compost, Bruce Coleman Limited **p13** Kjell B Sanved, Oxford Scientific Films **p14** C McDougal, Ardea London Ltd **p15** Marion Morrison, South American Pictures, (inset) Michael Fogden, Oxford Scientific Films **p16** A G (Bert) Wells, Oxford Scientific Films **p17** Eric Crichton, Bruce Coleman Limited **p18** Wardene Weisser, Ardea London Ltd **p19**

Andy Purcell, Bruce Coleman Limited **p20** (top) Treat Davidson, Frank Lane Picture Agency, (bottom) Phil Devries, Oxford Scientific Films **p21** J Cowan, Bruce Coleman Limited **p22** (top) Hans and Judy Beste, Oxford Scientific Films, (bottom) M P L Fogden, Oxford Scientific Films **p23** François Gohier, Ardea London Ltd **p24** Roberto Bunge, Ardea London Ltd **p25** P Morris, Ardea London Ltd **p26** Jeff Foott, Bruce Coleman Limited **p27** Andrew Plumptre, Oxford Scientific Films **p28** (top) M P L Fogden, Bruce Coleman Limited, (bottom) M P L Fogden, Bruce Coleman Limited **p29** (top) Starin, Ardea London Limited, (bottom) Michael Fogden, Oxford Scientific Films **p30** Michael Fogden, Oxford Scientific Films **p31** Carol Huges, Bruce Coleman Limited **p32** R A Acharya, Dinodia Picture Agency/Oxford Scientific Films **p33** (left) Peter Steyn, Ardea London Ltd, (right) M P L Fogden, Bruce Coleman Limited **p34** (top) Gryniewicz/ECOSCENE, (bottom) Michael Fogden, Oxford Scientific Films **p35** Philip Sharpe, Oxford Scientific Films **p36** C S Perkins, Magnum Photos **p37** J Hartley, Panos Pictures **p38** Michael K Nichols, Magnum Photos **p39** Marcos Santilli, Panos Pictures **p40** (left) John Mason, Ardea London Ltd, (right) Mark Edwards, Still Pictures **p41** ECOSCENE **p43** (top) Stephen Krasemann, Bruce Coleman Limited, (bottom left) ECOSCENE, (bottom right) Heather Angel **p44** Michael Fogden, Oxford Scientific Films

# Contents

# Introduction

The tropical rainforests are found in the hot, wet climate which occurs throughout much of the land that lies between the Tropics of Cancer and Capricorn. Altogether, tropical rainforests cover about 7 percent of the earth's land surface, which adds up to an area about the same size as the United States. Some parts of the world are particularly rich in rainforests. The Amazon basin has the largest block of rainforests in the world, with 2.31 million square miles of rainforest. This is more than all the other rainforests in the world put together. Two-thirds of the Amazonian rainforests are found in one country, Brazil. What happens in Brazil is, therefore, of the utmost importance for the future of tropical rainforests. Large and important rainforests are also found in Southeast Asia (particularly in Indonesia), central and West Africa, and also in parts of Australia and Papua New Guinea.

Part of the wonder and beauty of the tropical rainforests are in the rich variety of life that they contain. A staggering number of different kinds of plants and animals are linked together in complex and fascinating ways. At least half of the world's species of plants and animals live in rainforests. The Amazon rainforests, for example, are the habitat of over one quarter of the world's species of birds. A single acre of rainforest (the same size as two football fields) may contain over 200 species of trees and several hundred species of insects. In Europe and North America a similar area of forest may have less than a dozen species of trees.

Each year, however, an area about the size of England is stripped of its trees by **logging** and burning. Half of the world's tropical rainforests will have been converted to other uses by the year 2000. Thousands if not millions of species are disappearing before anyone has had a chance to collect and describe them.

The rainforests are also home to about 1,000 tribes of **indigenous people** who have learned to use the rainforests without causing long-lasting damage. The indigenous peoples have a wealth of

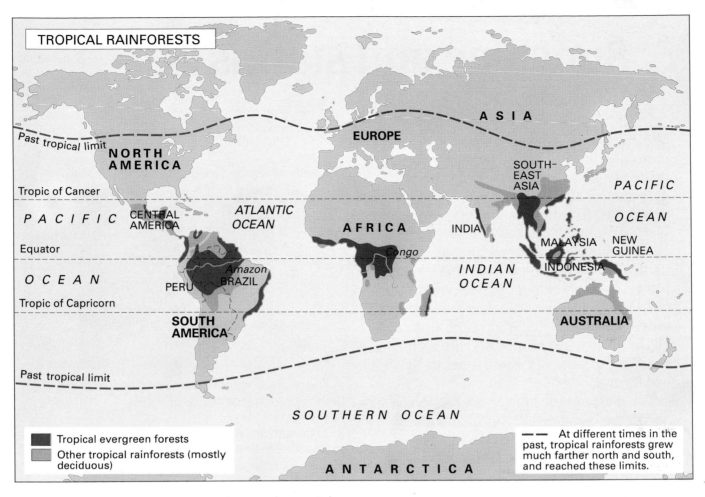

## TROPICAL RAINFORESTS

Past tropical limit

**NORTH AMERICA**

Tropic of Cancer

*PACIFIC*

CENTRAL AMERICA

*ATLANTIC OCEAN*

*AFRICA*

INDIA

**EUROPE**

**A S I A**

SOUTH-EAST ASIA

*PACIFIC*

*OCEAN*

MALAYSIA

NEW GUINEA

Equator

*OCEAN*

PERU

*Amazon* BRAZIL

*Congo*

INDONESIA

*INDIAN OCEAN*

Tropic of Capricorn

**SOUTH AMERICA**

**AUSTRALIA**

Past tropical limit

*S O U T H E R N   O C E A N*

◼ Tropical evergreen forests
◻ Other tropical rainforests (mostly deciduous)

– – – At different times in the past, tropical rainforests grew much farther north and south, and reached these limits.

**A N T A R C T I C A**

◁ Rainforests such as this one in Ecuador contain an astonishing variety of wildlife, from lantern bugs (below) to rafflesias (bottom), the largest flower in the world.

knowledge about rainforests and how the plants and animals can be used for food and as medicines. But they and their knowledge are also threatened by loss of their forest home.

Rainforests are also important for the part they play in moderating the earth's climate, protecting soils from heavy rainstorms, and helping to control flooding. The evaporation of water from the great mass of rainforest plants helps to spread moisture and warmth away from the equatorial regions to cooler parts. Everyone from the native Amazonian Indians to the inhabitants of the most modern concrete jungle has, therefore, a stake in the rainforests' future.

Words printed in **bold** are explained at the end of each section.

**logging**—cutting down trees for timber.
**indigenous people**—people who come from a country or region.

5

# Sunshine and storms

The climate near the equator is warm and moist all through the year so there are no proper seasons. In such a climate trees are able to grow all the time and they are always in leaf. The forests are, therefore, evergreen. The farther one travels away from the equator, however, the more the rain falls at particular times of the year. Where the year is divided into wet and dry seasons the trees are deciduous: They lose their leaves during the dry months. Deciduous rainforests (also called dry tropical rainforests) are found, for example, in parts of Central America, India, and Burma.

The height of the land above sea level affects the climate, and this in turn affects the type of rainforest that grows there. Rainfall increases and temperatures decrease the higher one goes up mountains, and the rainforest changes too. At higher levels it can be very cool. Here the forests are nearly always in cloud and are called cloud forests. On the really high mountains, such as the Andes, the temperatures eventually become too cold for trees to grow and the cloud forest gives way to scrub and grassland.

To some extent rainforests create their own climate. About half of the water that evaporates from rainforest plants falls back again as rain. The high rainfall is both a blessing and a curse for the rainforest plants. On the one hand it allows plants to grow for most, if not the whole, of the year but on the other it damages the soil and washes away valuable **nutrients**.

### Poor foundations

The richness of rainforests is built on surprisingly poor foundations. Most tropical soils are old—some over 100 million years old—and the combination of age, heat, and high rainfall has led to their mineral nutrients being leached (washed away).

How is it that rainforest plants are able to

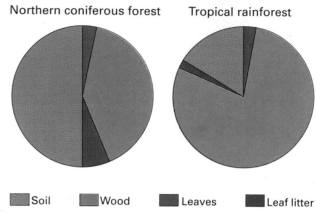

**MINERALS IN THE FOREST**

Northern coniferous forest    Tropical rainforest

☐ Soil    ☐ Wood    ☐ Leaves    ☐ Leaf litter

△ The charts show where mineral nutrients are held in two different kinds of forest.

▷ Little sunlight reaches the rainforest floor except where there are gaps in the canopy. Fungi (inset) thrive on the leaves that fall to the forest floor.

grow so well on such poor, infertile soils? Small amounts of minerals are found in the air and in rain, and plants are able to absorb these minerals. Some trees even grow fine roots through their bark to collect minerals. In the warm, moist climate there is less risk of damage from cold and fire, so the bark of most trees in the evergreen forests is thin. This makes it easier for roots, and even flowers, to grow through the bark.

As the trees grow they accumulate minerals in their wood. Most of the fertility of the rainforest is not in the soil but in the vegetation. This makes the rainforest a fragile habitat, for if the vegetation is destroyed the minerals which the trees and other plants need are soon washed away by the heavy rains.

## Ice age theories

We will only properly understand the rainforest and how to care for it when we understand its past. How has the rainforest, with its great variety of life, evolved? Part of the answer lies in the ice age.

## Refugia

The earth has been in an ice age for about the last 2 million years. Some scientists think that during the cold phases of the ice age the climate in the tropics was drier and that the rainforests retreated to a few areas where the climate or soils were wetter, such as in the foothills of the Andes and along the rivers. These areas became refuges, which scientists call **refugia**. Rainforests spread from the refugia as the climate improved and the tropics became wetter.

If this view is correct then the ice age refugia are the oldest and most stable areas of rainforest. Perhaps these are, therefore, the most important areas to save.

## Flooding

Other scientists have developed a very different theory about the history of rainforests. They believe that the rainforests of large basins such as the Amazon are affected in important ways by changes in water level and flooding.

For much of the last 100 million years sea levels have been higher than they are now and rivers were so large that much of the Amazon basin was a vast lake dotted with islands. Some scientists believe that rainforest plants and animals were more or less isolated on the islands, and that this encouraged the **evolution** of species peculiar to each island. When the sea level dropped as the ice sheets advanced, the rainforest spread from the islands to the land emerging from the retreating rivers and seas. With the changes in ice sheets and sea levels, this cycle could have been repeated several times over the last 2 million years.

Smaller, short-term changes could also have been caused by the annual floods. Sometimes these floods are catastrophic. Vast areas of rainforests are wiped out, the rivers cut new channels and old ones fill with mud and sand. Plants and animals colonize the new land until they are forced out by the next flood.

If this second theory is correct it means that the rainforest ecosystem, far from being stable for millions of years, has been disturbed. The disturbance may have been

△ A tree fern has been left standing in a cleared area of cloud forest in the Andes.

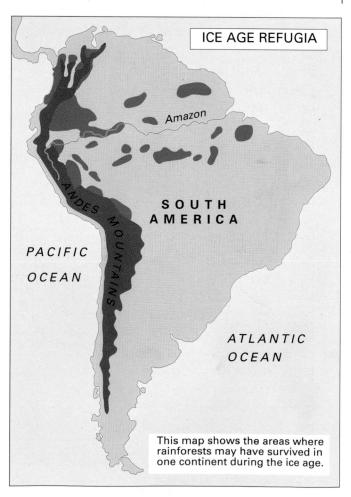

ICE AGE REFUGIA

This map shows the areas where rainforests may have survived in one continent during the ice age.

△ Rainforest rivers often flood during the rainy season.

important in the evolution of species as plants and animals adapted to new conditions.

### People

The indigenous people also disturb the forest by hunting animals, collecting plants, making clearings, and growing a wide variety of crops. This disturbance, far from being bad for the forest, may even be very good for it. By creating small areas of disturbance the rainforest as a whole is more varied. Different patches of the forests will have trees at different ages and different groupings of tree species, and these differences will in turn affect the kinds of foods and habitats available for animals.

If we follow the first theory based on refugia, we will see people as intruders in the forest who could damage it. If we follow the second theory based on disturbance, then we will see people as part of the forest with a key role to play in its evolution.

## Ecological services

Rainforests are important for protecting soils from **erosion**, reducing flooding, and the part they play in moderating the climate. We can think of these jobs as services to the environment, or as ecological services.

### Holding back the water

An important job all forests do is slowing the flow of water into rivers after heavy rains. This is particularly important in the tropics, where the rainfall is high and the rainstorms often violent. The forests act as sponges, holding back water and releasing it slowly into the streams and rivers. In forests, more water also soaks into the soil and is available for plants than in nonforested country. By slowing the speed that rainwater flows across the surface of the soil forests both protect the soil from erosion and moderate the changes in the level of rivers. By doing this forests reduce the suddenness and violence of floods.

The loss of forests has increased flooding in regions such as the floodplains of the Ganges in Bangladesh. The great Ganges has its source in the foothills and mountains of the Himalayas. From there it winds its way across a very fertile floodplain of Bangladesh toward the sea. Much of the forest that once clothed the steep mountain slopes has been lost through clearing for timber and fuelwood. When the heavy seasonal rains occur there is less of the "forest sponge" to soak up the rainwater, so the water runs off the land very quickly and makes any flooding much worse. Thousands of people are made homeless and millions of acres of farmland are drowned every time there is a major flood in the Ganges.

As important as these benefits of forests are to millions of people, the effect of rainforests on the world's climate could be even more important. Rainforests may well play an extremely important part in moderating the temperature changes of the earth's weather.

### Spreading the heat

When sunlight strikes the surface of the leaves of plants, the heat causes water in the leaves to evaporate. The heat energy that causes the water to evaporate does not disappear: It is stored in the water vapor as latent heat (hidden heat).

The water vapor from the plants rises until it condenses into water droplets. The condensing of water vapor into water droplets releases latent heat into the surrounding air and warms it. This takes place about six miles above the earth's surface. The warmed air is then pulled toward the poles by air pressure differences in the atmosphere. Thus heat energy that arrives at the earth's surface over the tropical rainforests is transferred to other parts of the world.

The loss of rainforest over large areas would reduce the amount of water that is evaporated in the tropics, which in turn would reduce the amount of heat that is pumped from the hot regions near the equator to cooler regions closer to the poles.

### Global warming

The other concern is the part rainforests play in preventing the earth's average temperature from rising higher than it is now. Some gases, particularly carbon dioxide, methane, and the CFCs used in refrigerators, help to trap heat within the earth's atmosphere—the so-called greenhouse effect. The higher the concentrations of these gases in the atmosphere the warmer the earth's climate will become.

The tropical rainforests are great stores of carbon. Plants take in carbon dioxide from the air and they use it to make food and substances such as wood. When a tree dies or is burned the carbon in its tissues is released back into the air in the form of carbon dioxide. If that tree is replaced by another, the new tree will, as it grows, absorb an equal amount of carbon dioxide

▽ Heavy rain falls on forest plants nearly every day in the tropics. Where forests have been cleared, the bare soil is eroded by the rain (right).

cloudiness will reflect more sunlight before it has a chance to warm the atmosphere.

Although the predictions are uncertain the important question to ask is: Do we want to take the chance of adding to the long-term damage to the climate by clearing rainforests? Would it not be better to play safe and keep our options open for the future? The countries that have to make the final decision on this are the countries that actually own the rainforests.

## Paying the price

If rainforests make the earth's climate more habitable and less extreme, then to some extent the rainforest-owning countries are subsidizing the rest of us. Is it fair to expect the people in those countries, most of whom are very poor, to bear all the costs of protecting their rainforests instead of logging them and making what money they can? And if we should all pay something to the cost of keeping rainforests protected for the future, how should everyone pay his or her share?

One way is being tried by a few electricity generating companies in the United States and the Netherlands. The companies intend to build more power stations to produce electricity and this will mean increasing the amount of coal they burn. The companies have plans to plant trees in the tropics, where trees grow faster than in colder climates, to absorb the carbon dioxide which will be produced by their power stations. The cost of this, eventually, will be passed on to the customers who buy electricity from them.

from the air. If, however, the total amount of the world's forest is decreased, huge amounts of carbon will be released as carbon dioxide into the air, where it will add to the amount of greenhouse gases present.

It has been estimated by some scientists that about one-fifth to one-third of the carbon dioxide being released comes from the burning of rainforests. In 1989 the burning of the Brazilian forests probably added 350 million tons of carbon to the air.

A doubling of the amount of carbon dioxide in the air is calculated to lead to about a 4.5°F rise in the average world temperature. This would be enough to cause the ice caps over Greenland and possibly Antarctica to melt, which in turn would cause sea levels to rise. Large parts of low-lying land around the world, much of which is very heavily populated, would be flooded.

Not all scientists agree that the earth's climate will become warmer due to greenhouse gases. It is possible that as the temperature rises, more water will evaporate from the oceans and the increase in

**nutrients**—mineral substances that plants need for nourishment.
**refugia**—places where plants and animals have not been affected by changes in climate that have happened in nearby areas.
**evolution**—a gradual change in animals or plants that helps them to survive in their environment.
**erosion**—the wearing away of soil, rock, sand, etc., usually by water, wind, or ice.

# The forest skyscraper

The rainforest consists of several layers of plants, in some ways similar to the floors in a skyscraper. Each layer is home to different animals. The top three layers are tree layers. Below them is a layer of shrubs and young trees, and beneath that is the forest floor. Each layer produces different foods which attract different animals.

However, in the evergreen forests very few shrub and herb plants are able to grow. The trees have leaves all year and block out most of the light. Only in the dry rainforests, where the trees lose all their leaves for part of the year, is there a dense undergrowth of shrubs. The shrubs support a range of animals that are not found in the evergreen rainforests.

## Up in the roof

The crowns (tops) of the taller trees form the forest canopy, up to 200 feet above the ground. Although the crowns are very close to each other, they are separated by a narrow gap. The gaps probably help to prevent diseases spreading from one tree to another and make it more difficult for tree-damaging animals to travel from tree to tree. However, nonflying animals have solved this problem in different ways. Some, such as the gliding squirrels, have developed a flap of skin between their front and back legs which allows them to glide across gaps.

The canopy acts as the roof of the forest. It stops sunlight from reaching the forest floor and moisture from escaping. The result is a twilit, warm, damp environment below the canopy in which few plants can grow but which is ideal for the growth of fungi and bacteria. Most rainforest animals, from tiny

▽ The giant flying squirrel can glide between the trees in the canopy.

△ The pool of water in this cup-of-flame bromeliad may support many tiny creatures.

insects to sloths, live in the canopy, for this is where most of the flowers, fruits, seeds, and leaves on which they feed are produced.

The canopy is also home to epiphytes. Epiphytes are plants which live on other plants but do not damage them. Many perch on trees and absorb water either straight from the air or from the bark of trees.

Epiphytes are very important in the life of the forest because by absorbing minerals they increase the fertility of the forest. Some of the minerals taken in by the epiphytes are absorbed by the trees when the epiphytes die and decay. Some epiphytes, such as the bromeliads of South America (relatives of the pineapple), collect water in leaves shaped like containers. The containers form miniature ponds in the treetops, in which insects and frogs raise their young.

## Above the rooftops

Here and there a few species of trees pierce through the forest canopy. These trees are called emergents because their crowns emerge above the main canopy. This gives them the advantage of being able to get more light than the plants lower down.

◁ Few plants can grow in the darkness beneath the canopy of trees. Low-growing shrubs and ground plants can only flourish in sunny clearings and at forest edges.

However, there is a price to pay for this advantage, for above the main canopy the air moves faster than in the forest and moving air evaporates water from leaves faster than still, humid air does. To save water the emergent trees have small, leathery leaves. They are also more likely than shorter trees to be struck by lightning in the fierce tropical storms. The emergent trees have little need to attract animals as most of them use the wind to carry their pollen and to disperse their seeds. Large birds of prey such as the harpy eagle of South America use the emergent trees as nesting sites and as lookouts (see page 33).

### The lower roof

Beneath the main canopy some smaller trees, such as palm trees, thrive in the damp air and dim light. The trees that grow at this level have large, often very long leaves to absorb as much light as possible. In the still, humid air, water does not evaporate quickly from their large leaves.

Many of the animals found in the main canopy will also be seen lower down, but leaf-eating animals often prefer the lower layers because the leaves are larger and less poisonous. The lower canopy is also the habitat for many types of birds, particularly those species adapted to feed on the insects living on the trunks of trees.

## Down in the shrubbery

The shrub layer is even darker than the lower canopy, and plants are sparse. However, gaps are formed when the taller canopy trees die or storms blow trees over. The shrub plants are among the pioneers in any gap or clearing that is made in the forest. Eventually they are crowded out by the growing canopy trees but for a time they can grow in large numbers. At this stage they act as nurse plants, protecting the tree seedlings until they grow above the shrubs.

Shrub plants are food for deer, buffalo, and tapirs which eat the young leaves and shoots. The large apes, such as the orangutan of Asia and the gorilla of Africa, are restricted to these lower levels of the forest by their heavy weight.

### The ground floor

Dead plant and animal material decays very fast in rainforests. The warm, damp conditions are ideal for the growth of fungi, bacteria, and small animals such as termites which cause decay. The rainforest trees have a vast network of fine roots close to the surface of the soil which quickly take up the nutrients released by the decaying plants.

Where gaps have formed, sunlight streams through to the forest floor. In these sunny spots there is, for a while at least, a rich growth of grasses and young shrubs on which larger mammals, such as the deer, tapir, and duiker antelope can feed. These large mammals are the main food of the carnivores (meat-eating animals), such as the American jaguar and the Asian tiger. The animals that we find living in rainforests are, therefore, related to its structure.

▷ Lianas are carried up to the light on trees. The canopy vegetation helps to keep the air in the forest damp. Leaf frogs (inset) thrive in the moist atmosphere.

▽ Orangutans live in the rainforests of Asia.

# The rainforest community

The millions of species of plants and animals living in rainforests are not just a collection of species living separate, unconnected lives. Each one has become adapted to carry out a particular job in the life of the forest. There is much still to be learned about the relationships among plants and animals but enough is known to make us realize how complex they are.

Rainforest animals play a vital role in the reproduction of rainforest plants. More than in any other ecosystem animals are important for plant pollination, partly because there is very little wind and partly because trees of the same species are widely spaced. In other ecosystems it is the wind that carries the pollen of many of the plants.

Reproduction for flowering plants involves two major steps. The first one is to produce seeds and the second one is to spread them widely through the forest in the hope that some will be able to grow into new plants. A seed is produced when a pollen grain fertilizes (joins with) an egg. An egg can usually only be fertilized by pollen from a flower on another plant of the same species. So plants have to transfer their pollen to other flowers of their own kind, often between plants that are widely separated.

Good pollinators must be strong fliers able to feed over long distances, for this will increase the chance of a plant transferring its pollen to the flowers of other plants of its species. Birds, bats, hawk moths, and large bees are the most common pollinators.

▷ The brightly colored passion flower attracts birds.
▽ Hawk moths can hover to feed.

16

Plants reward them with a supply of nectar, a sugary liquid which is very high in energy. The animals are attracted to the flowers by the food and they unintentionally carry pollen from flower to flower.

**Design for success**

The plants have several ways of making sure the pollinating animals will carry their pollen to others of their kind and not waste too much of the pollen by visiting other plant species. One of these ways is to attract the attention of particular groups of animals.

For example, birds have a very poor sense of smell but are attracted to harsh and contrasting colors. Bird-pollinated flowers produce no scent but have bright colors such as red. Bees, on the other hand, are attracted to flowers that are weakly scented and have lively colors such as blue and yellow.

Flowers pollinated by the night-flying bats and moths are white or creamy and they produce powerful scents and odors which help the pollinating animals to find the flowers in the dark. Most of the bat- and moth-pollinated flowers only open at night.

This matching of a plant species to a particular animal group increases the chance of pollen being carried between flowers of the same species. Each flower only provides a visiting animal with a small amount of the food it needs. This increases the chance of the pollinating animals moving to other flowers in search of more food.

In the evergreen tropical rainforests there is no need for all tree species to flower at the same time, because there are no seasons. Plants therefore do not have to compete for the same pollinating animals: Different species can flower at different times. This lessens the chance that pollen will be carried from the flowers of one species to those of different species.

▷ The tailed jay, like other butterflies, sits on the flower to feed.

▽ Hummingbirds have long, curved bills that fit inside tube-shaped flowers on which they feed.

Many flowers are made in such a way that only a certain group of animals, or in some cases only a single species, can reach their nectar. In the American rainforests hummingbirds are the largest and most important group of bird pollinators. Their narrow, curved bills are shaped to fit inside the tubes of flowers that they visit.

Hummingbirds often have a set route through the forest, sometimes called a trapline, which they fly every day, visiting the plants as they come into flower. In Africa and Asia the place of hummingbirds is taken by sunbirds, while in Australia and New Guinea honeyeaters are the main bird pollinators. These birds also have narrow, curved bills. These similar adaptations to suit the same sort of feeding methods are examples of **convergent evolution**.

It is only in the tropics that bats have become adapted to feed on nectar, and many rainforest trees rely on them for pollination. Parkias are a major group of plants adapted to use bats as pollinators.

They produce clusters of flowers which hang down on long stalks beneath the canopy. The bats are able to approach the flowers from beneath without damaging their wings on the leaves and branches of trees.

The stamens on which the pollen is borne are massed together like the hairs of a shaving brush. As the bats land to drink the nectar their breasts are dusted with pollen. This is then carried to the next flower cluster that the bats visit.

Moths have very long tongues which can reach down into long flower tubes. They hover beside flowers to probe deep inside the tubes to reach nectar (see pages 16 and 20). Butterflies also have long tongues but, unlike the moths, they are light enough to stand on the flowers while they drink the nectar. Butterflies are particularly important pollinators of the vines, common plants in the rainforests. The vines produce trumpet-shaped flowers, with the nectar in a narrow tube. The design of the flower prevents bees from reaching the nectar unless they bite through the side of the flower tube. The chances are that only butterflies will be able to land, reach the nectar, and incidentally pick up the pollen.

## A three-way partnership

Just as plants are dependent upon certain animals for pollination, so the animals are dependent upon particular groups of plants for their food. This two-way dependence is called **interdependence** and is an important feature of tropical rainforests.

Nowhere is the idea of interdependence better shown than in the three-way relationship of orchid bees, bee orchid plants, and the brazil nut tree. The brazil nut tree is very valuable in the Amazonian forests and many people make their living by collecting and selling the nuts. The tree depends for its pollination on both the orchid plant, which grows as an epiphyte (see page 13) in the tree canopy, and the orchid bee.

The brazil nut tree's flowers have a hood which protects the parts inside. Only large bees such as female orchid bees are strong enough to push the hood back. As the bees lift the hood, their backs are dusted with pollen which they then carry from flower to flower. The male bees, on the other hand, visit bee orchid flowers to collect fragrant chemicals, which they use to attract female bees for mating. As they collect the chemicals they also pick up pollen which they carry to other orchid flowers.

The brazil nut tree, the orchid plant, and orchid bees are all dependent on one another. If any one of them disappears from the forest the other two will not be able to reproduce.

In Brazil, even where ranchers have a license to burn rainforest, they are supposed to make sure that the brazil nut trees are left unharmed, because of the value of nuts to the economy of the Amazon region. However, protecting the brazil nut trees will only be useful if the bee orchid plant and the orchid bee are also protected. Until we know much more about complex relationships such as this we need to be very careful how we use the tropical rainforests. Otherwise we may accidentally destroy other animal and plant partnerships.

△ Humming hawk moth

▷ Rainforest orchids are often scented and brightly colored to attract insects.

▽ Different species of orchid bees are attracted to different bee orchids.

# Orchids

The part that orchids play in the life of tropical rainforests is not fully understood, but it is almost certainly one of great importance. Many orchids are epiphytes.

In the tropics the number of species of orchids is immense. There are more species of orchids in Central and South American rainforests than there are species of trees, herbs, and grasses in all of Europe.

The unusual feature of orchids is that many of the species can only be pollinated by a single species of insect. Most other rainforest flowering plants make use of a particular group of animals such as bees, birds, or bats, but very few of them depend on a single species of animal. We urgently need to understand the characteristics of orchids so that we know better how to manage the tropical rainforests.

**convergent evolution**—the development of certain similarities in unrelated animals that live in similar environments.
**interdependence**—the relationships between two or more plants or animals, in which each relies on the other for life.

21

# Spreading the seeds

## Fruit for the animals

Just as some animals spread pollen, others play a vital role in the life of rainforests by dispersing (spreading) seeds. Seed dispersal, unlike pollination, is a chance event for most plants. There is no guarantee that their seeds will be dropped in places where they can germinate and grow into mature plants. So plants have to produce large numbers of seeds and spread them across the forest in the hope that some will land in suitable places.

△ Black flying fox bat

▽ Ginger plants can grow in the shade on the rainforest floor.

△ Squirrel monkeys eat mostly fruit. They like large, brightly colored fruits best.

To attract seed-dispersing animals, plants produce tasty, fleshy fruits. The seeds stick to the fruit's flesh so that when an animal eats the flesh it also swallows the seeds, which then lie in its digestive system without being digested. Eventually the seeds are expelled, and if the conditions are suitable they will germinate and a few may grow into mature plants.

The good seed-dispersers are animals that roam long distances through the forest, as this increases the chance that seeds will be spread widely. Some of the monkeys and apes, and large birds such as toucans and hornbills, are especially important seed-dispersers.

Many of the plants have fruits which are particularly attractive to certain groups of animals. Apes and monkeys, for example, like to eat sweet fruits that hang down from branches, because they can reach such fruits easily with their hands. The fruits of mahogany trees, which occur widely in Asia, have sweet-tasting flesh which is rich in energy and protein. Gibbons travel long distances in the canopy, using an overarm method to swing from branch to branch in search of such fruits.

**Bats**
Fruit-eating bats are responsible for the dispersal of many tropical seeds. Bats prefer fruits that are held well away from the leaves and branches, as they are on the palms, so they can approach them without damaging their wings on the leaves of the trees. Fruits that attract bats often have a musty or cheesy smell. The fruits are carried by the bats to their roosting sites, where they tear the flesh from the seed. Some species of flying fox bats have a huge wing span—up to 5 feet. The large bats can carry fruit weighing about 7 ounces.

Bats also take fruits containing small seeds, such as the squashy fruits of fig trees. The bats press the fruits against the tops of their mouths to extract the juice. There are many kinds of fig trees, and at any time during the year there are always some trees producing fruit. This means that they are a very reliable source of food for bats; they can be eaten at times when few other plants are producing fruit. In fact, almost any fruit-eating animal will take figs when other fruits are not available.

## Birds

The toucans of Central and South American rainforests eat large fruits, especially those containing only a single seed. Only the flesh of the fruit is digested; the seed is either spat out again or it passes through the bird's digestive system. In the time that it takes for the seed to be expelled the bird is likely to have moved some distance through the forest, and in this way the seeds are spread over a wide area. In Africa and in Asia the place of toucans is taken by hornbills. Although hornbills are not closely related to toucans they are also large birds that eat similar types of foods and have similar shaped bills.

Another group of seed-dispersing birds are pigeons. Pigeons are plump, medium-size birds found throughout the world, including our largest cities. Most species of pigeons are seed-eating birds of open woodlands and grasslands but a few are adapted to feed on rainforest fruits, particularly in Southeast Asia and Australia. In Australian coastal rainforests the red-crowned and wompoo pigeons are quite common and the distinctive Torres Strait pigeon migrates from New Guinea to northern Australia for the spring and summer.

Although smaller than most toucans and hornbills, fruit-eating pigeons can also carry seeds a considerable distance before expelling them. Like many birds, pigeons are attracted to fruits with brilliant contrasting colors—usually red, black, or yellow. Such fruits are adapted to be seen at a distance among the green background of the canopy leaves.

△ The macaw can crack very hard nutshells with its strong beak.

▷ The quetzal is an endangered species.

Many of the fruit-eating animals eat a wide variety of fruits. The quetzal bird of Central America depends entirely on the fruits of the wild avocado tree and is this tree's main seed-disperser. The tree is therefore also dependent on the quetzal and this relationship is another fascinating example of interdependence. The loss of wild avocado trees by rainforest logging is threatening the quetzal with extinction.

Unlike all these birds, parrots are seed destroyers, not seed dispersers. They eat and digest the seed itself rather than the fruit, so they prevent the seeds from spreading. Large parrots such as the macaw parrots of the Central and South American rainforests are able to hold fruits down on branches with their claws while they strip away the flesh with their beaks. Once the seed is exposed parrots can use their large strong beaks to crack the coats of the seeds.

## Mistletoes

Seed dispersal is a chance event for most plants but one exception is the mistletoes. Mistletoes are **parasites** of trees and they grow on branches and tap into the trees' sap. The mistletoe bird eats the fruits of the

mistletoe plant. The mistletoe seeds contain irritant substances which make the birds rub their backsides on tree branches to get rid of the irritation. When they rub they deposit the seeds exactly where they have a good chance of gaining a foothold.

## Fish that eat fruit

In many parts of the Amazon fruit-eating fish are highly prized by people who live along the rivers. Overfishing is reducing some populations of these fish, and their loss could well threaten the existence of trees like the *Eperua*. The *Eperua* tree grows beside the rainforest rivers and produces pods that explode when the seeds inside are ripe. The explosion scatters the seeds into the water where they are swallowed by the tambaqui fish. The fish may carry the seeds a long way upstream before some are expelled. When the river floods, some of the expelled seeds settle and grow on the riverbank.

Important fisheries are in turn being threatened by the loss of rainforests beside rivers. When the trees that overhang the water are cut down, the fruits on which many of the fish feed are lost.

▽ Some fish feed on fruits that fall from trees growing beside rivers in rainforests.

△ A female buffalo with her calf

## The bulldozer herbivores

Elephants are found in the Asian and African rainforests and, together with buffalo, they push over trees and shrubs as they wander through the forest. The clearings produced by their bulldozing activities increase the numbers of habitats for grazing animals such as antelope and deer.

Elephants and buffalo are **herbivores** and eat the fruits of several types of rainforest trees. The seeds can lie in their digestive systems unharmed for a week or more before they are expelled, and because these animals can travel long distances in a day the seeds can be spread over a very large area.

Elephants and buffalo are not restricted to the rainforest but usually wander between it and the neighboring grasslands. Seeds from rainforest plants may be expelled during visits to the grassland. If the seeds germinate and grow into trees, other fruit-eating animals, such as hornbills, will come and perch in the branches. Soon a whole host of seeds belonging to many species of plants are being expelled onto the ground nearby and some will germinate and grow under the protection of the first trees. In this way large herbivores can play an important role in expanding the area of rainforest.

## Help from horses

Knowledge of the role of large plant-eating mammals in seed dispersal has been put to good use in western Costa Rica in Central America. In what is now the Santa Rosa National Park, large areas of grassland were left from when the rainforests had been cleared for cattle ranches. The grasslands within the national park are now abandoned and the park managers want rainforests to regrow on the cleared lands. Central America has no bulldozer herbivores such as the elephant or buffalo, but there are horses on the neighboring ranches. The horses were introduced from Spain 400 years ago and are not wild animals native to the Costa Rican rainforest, but they play a role that once belonged to a large animal that is now extinct.

The park managers have allowed horses from the nearby ranches to feed and rest in the forest, where they swallow seeds of trees and shrubs as they graze and browse. When the horses move back out on to the grasslands they eventually expel the seeds, which are conveniently provided with a good ration of manure. Once a tree becomes established in the grasslands, birds such as toucans roost and feed in its canopy, and soon they, too, are expelling seeds of yet more rainforest plants. Within a few years islands of rainforests appear in the grassland. As these islands grow and join with their neighbors the forest rapidly expands.

The Santa Rosa success has an important lesson for conservationists and nature lovers the world over. It shows that we must allow ourselves to think flexibly and not close our minds to ideas just because they seem to be unnatural. Even though the Santa Rosa horses are introduced from another country they perform a useful job in helping the rainforest to regenerate.

**parasite**—a plant or animal that lives and feeds on another.
**herbivores**—animals that feed on plants.

27

# Chemical warfare

The seeds and leaves of plants are rich sources of food for many kinds of animals. If plants had no way of protecting their seeds and leaves from being eaten none would survive and they would in time become extinct. Plants have to protect themselves against the plant predators and there are many ways they can do this. One of the most important ways is to produce poisons and other chemicals which deter the plant predators and limit the damage they can do. Many plants around the world do this but it is in the tropical rainforests that chemical defense reaches its greatest heights.

Plants often coat their seeds in poisons. Seed-eating animals have to make the poisons harmless before they can digest the seed. Plants of different species will use different poisons, so that although a seed-eating animal may evolve a way of making one or more of the poisons harmless it is unlikely to be able to make all the poisons produced by all the plants harmless. Most plants also lace their leaves with poisons. The rainforest is, in fact, the scene of a continuous chemical warfare between plants and animals which, after

△ Katydids, usually camouflaged as leaves, feed on plants.

▽ Most plants protect their leaves with poisons.

△ Colobus monkeys can eat poisonous leaves quite safely.

millions of years of evolution, has reached a kind of truce.

The battles follow a set pattern. A plant species is attacked by herbivorous animals. In time it evolves a poison which deters the herbivores from eating it. Then at least one species of animal evolves a way of making the poison harmless. No animal species has yet evolved a way of making all the plant poisons harmless, so we have a great variety of plant species, each being eaten by only one, or at the most a few, animal species. Plant predators come in all shapes and sizes. The larger ones, such as monkeys, tend to eat a little bit from many different kinds of plants and, therefore, swallow only small quantities of many different poisons, while smaller ones, such as beetles, are adapted to feed on only one kind of plant.

### Monkey tricks

Some species of monkey are well adapted to feed on seeds or leaves. The Uakaris monkey, which lives in the rainforests beside some of the tributaries of the Amazon, has teeth specially adapted to crack open the hard shells of seeds. The Yanomami Indians have used this monkey as food for centuries but sadly it has now become endangered since the Yanomami lands have been invaded by gold miners hungry for meat.

The howler monkey, which is also found in the Central and South American rainforests, lives in large groups among the lower canopy and understory trees where the leaves are less poisonous than in higher parts of the canopy. It has a large sac attached to its stomach in which the leaves of rainforest trees ferment.

The monkeys best adapted for feeding on plant leaves, however, are the colobus monkeys, which live in the African rainforests. Their stomachs produce a broth which makes the poisons in leaves harmless as soon as they are swallowed.

### Insects on the warpath

There are many insects which feed on plants: leaf eaters, sap suckers, pollen raiders, and seed predators. The variety of insects in rainforests is difficult to imagine, as the number of species is huge. Scientists have counted over 900 species on one tree.

▽ Some beetles feed on leaves.

Although plants are well armed against insect attack the insects, too, have been successful in the chemical counterattack. Aphids, for example, plug into the veins that carry sap from the plant's leaves to its roots. Plants lace their sap with toxins to deter insects, so aphids can only feed on plants whose poisons they can make harmless. Some aphids, however, not only can make these toxins harmless but also can store them in their own bodies as defense against animals such as spiders and ladybird beetles which hunt them.

Adult butterflies and moths play a vital role in the pollination of many plants but the young stage, the larva or caterpillar, is a voracious plant eater, particularly of leaves. The larva of each species of butterfly and moth is able to counter the poison produced by at least one plant and, like the aphids, many of the larvae are able to store and use the plant poisons for their own protection against predators such as birds.

## Chemical cures

There is a tremendous variety of chemicals within the rainforest and by trial and error the native peoples have learned how to use many of them for their own benefit. So far, however, scientists have investigated only 1 percent of the plant species available. About 40 percent of our drugs have their origins in plants and with such a large variety of plants available in the tropical forests we just do not know what might be found in the future. The National Cancer Institute in the United States is already collecting plant material from rainforests around the world and extracting chemicals to see if any have uses in curing cancer.

## The spacing of plants

Trees of the same species do not normally grow close to each other in a rainforest. Many may be at least 300 feet away from another of the same kind. Why is this so?

When a tree drops its seeds, seed eaters eat most of them. If any seeds do manage to grow into seedlings the leaf eaters will eat the leaves and kill the seedlings. Usually a seed can only escape the notice of animals by being carried a long distance from the parent tree, away from the animals adapted to eat them. The fruit-eating animals, such as birds and bats, are important seed carriers (see page 22).

◁ The wood-boring beetle feeds on nectar, but its larvae feed on twigs, roots, shoots, and dead wood.

▷ The caterpillars of butterflies and moths feed on plants.

# Teeth, claws, and more

While most animals eat plants, some eat other animals. The animal predators range in size from insects, spiders, frogs, snakes, and chameleon lizards to the mighty tiger of Asia. Whatever the size of the predators they are usually fewer in number than the species on which they prey and they usually need a great deal more living space.

The largest predators, such as the tiger and jaguar, are useful **indicator species**. They are at the top of the food chain, and if their populations are doing well we can be reasonably sure that the forests are in good shape. Any problems such as loss of forest habitat or a major decrease in their prey will affect the large predators. If we can set aside forest reserves large enough to protect animals such as the tiger and jaguar, we will also be protecting many species that need less living space.

## The big cats

Several species of wild cats live in rainforests and are well adapted for hunting in forests. They have very sharp claws which can be withdrawn into protective sheaths.

▷ The tiger is one of the largest predators found in rainforests. Its striped coat helps to camouflage the animal when it moves through the trees.

This allows cats to walk silently and also prevents the claws from becoming blunt. The claws can then be used as very efficient daggers for wounding prey. Many of the wild cats have striped or dappled coats which provide excellent camouflage among the moving leaves of the forest undergrowth, especially as the light is usually very dim when the cats are out hunting.

In Asia the tiger is the largest and most powerful cat. It prefers the dense undergrowth to the more open forests. It is therefore more likely to be found in the dry, seasonal rainforests, where there is a better-developed shrub layer, than in the evergreen rainforests.

A fully grown, healthy tiger is capable of killing animals the size of buffalo, although the more usual prey is deer, antelopes, and wild pigs. Tigers do farmers a service by killing such animals, which are pests because they raid farmers' crops. However, some tigers develop a habit of killing stock and a few also attack people. Such animals are a serious danger to local villagers and tourists.

△ Bird-eating spiders spin webs in which hummingbirds sometimes get caught by accident. The spider then sucks its victim's body liquids.

◁ Birds of prey such as the crowned eagle nest in the forest canopy.

Ideally the conservation of the tiger requires large areas of forest so the animals are able to find all the food and living space they need in the wild. If the animals have to venture out of the forest and on to farmland they are likely to come into conflict with humans by killing stock and even people.

In Central and South America the tiger's counterpart is the jaguar. Although not as large as most tigers, it weighs about the same as a very large human (250 pounds).

The jaguar can climb in the canopy of the forest and is quite capable of leaping from branch to branch, so canopy-dwelling animals, such as sloths and spider monkeys, are not entirely safe. However, its favorite food is the peccary, a member of the pig family. It also hunts along rivers for alligators and the capybara, which is the largest rodent in the world. Like the tiger, jaguars need a lot of living room and the large Manu National Park in eastern Peru is a particularly important reserve for them (see page 43).

Smaller, even more agile cats, such as the ocelot and the margay cat, hunt in the top canopy for birds, snakes, and lizards. Some of the wild cats are threatened with extinction. As the rainforests are cut down the cats are losing their habitat, and they are also being hunted illegally for their skins. The rarer the animals become the more the price of their skins increases, and hunters are prepared to take even more risks to kill the animals that remain.

## Birds of prey

Some of the most powerful and successful animal predators are the eagles. Each major rainforest region has its own species. In South America we find the harpy eagle, in Asia the monkey-eating eagle, and in Africa the crowned eagle. These large birds perch on the tall emergent trees of the forest, from where they swoop down on unsuspecting animals such as sloths and monkeys feeding or resting in the canopy.

# Amphibians and reptiles

Rainforests are home to many species of frogs (which are amphibians), snakes and lizards (which are reptiles), all of which eat other animals. Amphibians and reptiles are cold-blooded, backboned animals. Cold-blooded animals are not able to keep their body temperatures at certain levels. The temperature of most tropical rainforests is just about the right level for them. Amphibians also have moist skins and the high humidity of rainforests prevents the skin from drying out. Most species also need to raise their young, the tadpoles, in water.

Frogs mostly hunt insects, which they catch with their tongues. Insects are found at all levels of the rainforest and many frogs are found in the forest canopy. Here, finding large pools of water for the tadpoles can be a problem. Fortunately, the stores of water in bromeliads are useful for this purpose (see page 13). Frogs are themselves hunted by many other kinds of predators such as herons, egrets, and snakes. Some species of

△ The chameleon is a sure-footed lizard of the forest.

▽ Many arrow poison frogs lay their eggs on land. When the tadpoles hatch the female carries them up a tree and drops them into a pool of water in a bromeliad plant, where the tadpoles develop into frogs.

frogs, such as the arrow poison frogs of South America, protect themselves by producing powerful nerve poisons in the skin.

Rainforest reptiles are more independent of water than amphibians. Their eggs have a waterproof covering and the young do not have to be raised in water. The animals also have a dry skin which does not have to be kept moist.

The chameleon lizard is extremely well adapted for life in the treetops. It can grip branches very firmly with its tail and feet. Once in place it shoots out its long tongue to catch insects which come into range. It can also change its color. For camouflage it is a mottle of green and brown but if threatened it can change its color to a startling combination of blue and crimson.

Snakes are also well adapted for hunting in the forest canopy. They climb and move about quietly, able when necessary to stay stock still. Snakes kill their prey in one of two ways. Some species such as the vipers use poison. They bite their victim with their fangs, which inject the poison. The boas, on the other hand, strangle their prey by wrapping part of their body around it.

Parrot snake

## Tapping the flow
A few animals obtain nourishment from other animals without killing them. Some ants use sap-feeding aphids much as we use dairy cows to supply us with milk. The aphids plug into the veins of a plant. The rush of sap, rich in sugars, is more than the aphid can use and some of the sugar passes through its digestive system undigested. The ants feed on the sugar as it is released from the aphid.

**indicator species** —plants or animals that are studied to check the state of a particular environment. If a chosen species is thriving, its habitat is probably healthy.

# Farming the forests

About 1,000 indigenous tribes live in the world's tropical forests. In the South American Amazon there is, for example, the Yanomami, in Africa the Baku, and in Southeast Asia the Penans. The earliest rainforests to be settled were the Southeast Asian forests some 40,000 years ago. The Amazonian forests were not occupied by American Indians until much later, probably some 6,000 years ago.

The very fact that tropical rainforests exist despite the fact that people have lived in them for thousands of years suggests that the indigenous people have learned to use the rainforests without causing long-term damage. For that the rest of the world owes them a big debt; for, as we are finding out, this environment is easily damaged unless it is treated with care and understanding.

### Hunters and gatherers

How have the indigenous people managed to look after the rainforest while making a living from it? Different tribes have different ways of using the forests. Some are entirely hunters and food gatherers. Many, though, make a living by both hunting and growing crops. Most of the tribes depend to some extent upon wild game, fish, and wild plants. They know which fruits and nuts are good to eat, which plants can be used as medicines, and which plants produce poisons that are useful in hunting and fishing.

In many tribes plants, animals, and landscape features such as hills and lakes are thought to have spirits. If they are offended these spirits may bring bad luck in hunting, or bring on illness or some other problem which the offender will live to regret. Such beliefs bind each person of a tribe to the other members and to the forest and the life in it.

△ The Yanomami hunt animals and gather fruits, but they also grow crops in clearings in the forest.

▷ Large areas of rainforest are burned by local farmers to clear land for growing crops. The system is called slash-and-burn agriculture.

### Farmers

The Yanomami is a tribe that grows crops, hunts wild game, and collects wild plants. It is the largest indigenous tribe in Brazil. Their farming or gardening, like that of many indigenous people, copies many of the features of the natural forests. The gardening cycle begins with the Yanomami cutting trees to create a garden plot. The plots are only about the same size as the gaps which form naturally in forests in storms. The clearing work is done in the dry season and the leaves and wood are left to dry. Toward the end of the dry season the dried plants are burned. The ash is rich in nutrients which enriches the soil. The Yanomami plant their crops as soon as the wet season begins.

They grow some 60 or so crops altogether. The plants fall into four groups and each group matures at a different time. Corn takes about 4 months, sweet potatoes around 6 months, and cassava, banana, and plantains 9 to 10 months. The longest maturing group is the tree crops, such as pejibage palms, which take about 3 years

but which go on producing food for 10 years. Most of the plants are grown mixed together. The bananas, papayas, and palms protect the corn and sweet potatoes from the sun and heavy rains, and by growing several crops together insect damage is kept to a minimum.

The plots are usually abandoned after three years, when the gardens need more time and effort spent on them as the fertility leaches away. But the families can return for up to 10 years to collect the fruits of the palms. However, the plots have to be left for at least 50 years before they can be cleared and farmed again, for this is the time it takes for the forest which colonizes the abandoned clearings to replace the nutrients.

The Yanomami also hunt a large number of animal species. Macaw parrots, toucans, capybara, agoutis, deer, and peccaries are all eaten. Deer and peccaries spend much of their time feeding in forest clearings so the abandoned clearings create habitats for these animals. The Indians also make their bow strings from fibers collected from cecropia tress. The cecropia tree is a fast-growing colonizer of forest clearings and so the garden plots are usually invaded by this species of tree.

The increase in population of nonindigenous forest people, particularly in Africa and Southeast Asia, has led to colonization of rainforests. In many cases the forest is not given time to recover its fertility before crops are grown again. This means that unless the farmers can afford to buy fertilizers the forest land will eventually be too poor to grow crops.

The problems in saving rainforests for the future are different in different parts of the world. In some places forests are lost because of logging. In some places people are searching for land to farm. In countries such as Brazil the government has encouraged wealthy individuals and companies to settle the "frontier" regions of the country, which include the Amazonian rainforests. Vast areas are cleared for short-term gains (see page 38).

# Rainforests of the future

We will only arrive at the best solutions for saving rainforests if we understand correctly the reasons for their loss. Increasing populations, large international debts, and demands for wood (for building and for fuel) are usually given as the main reasons. But also important are the attitudes of governments and people in the rainforest-owning countries.

For example, the Brazilian government has encouraged the settlement of large areas of forest by ranchers. To claim ownership of government-owned land a person or company has to show that the land is being used effectively. The quickest and cheapest way to claim land is to burn the forest and create cattle pasture. This has been the major cause of the clearing of rainforest in the Amazon basin. However, most of the ranches have been abandoned after only five to six years, because they have lost their fertility. During the working life of the average Amazonian ranch each square yard of pasture has produced just enough beef for three quarter-pound hamburgers!

One of the other causes for rainforest loss has been the movement of small farmers into the forest in search of land. If the tropical countries carried out land reform they could help more small farmers to stay on land outside of the rainforest. At the moment a small number of landowners own most of the land, which makes it difficult for small farmers to own or rent land.

▽ Most of the land that is burned and cleared in Amazonia is used for cattle pasture.

△ Huge areas of rainforest are cleared every year to provide timber.

# Tropical woods

Logging has caused a lot of damage to the rainforests of Southeast Asia and Africa but so far has not been the main cause for the loss of rainforests in Central and South America. The American tropics only supply one-fifth of the timber cut from tropical rainforests. But as timber runs out in Southeast Asian and African forests, buyers are looking more and more to the forests of Central and South America for their timber. This could be a threat in the future unless the logging is carefully managed.

Some scientists believe it is not possible to log large areas of rainforest without damaging the forest habitat. Each tree removed means loss of nutrients and the removal of particular species of trees may upset the finely balanced relationships between plants and animals (see page 21 on orchids).

## Planting for profit

Despite this gloomy outlook for rainforests and logging, there are a few rays of hope that the situation can be improved. There may be ways of managing rainforests for timber production which take account of the needs of pollinating and seed-dispersing animals so the rainforests are able to regrow after some of the trees have been removed.

In an experiment in Peru, for example, trees are felled in narrow strips between 65 and 150 feet wide. These strips are no wider than many of the clearings produced naturally in the forest by storms and most seed-dispersing animals will cross a narrow strip between their food trees and drop seeds on the way.

The experiments show that after three or four years there is a rich undergrowth in the felled strips. The plan is to log each strip every 30 or 40 years. The advantage of strip felling for timber production is that the trees that grow in the strips are all the same age, which should make the later fellings more efficient and profitable. In natural forests only a few trees in an area are usually at the right age for logging and this means loggers have to search large areas of forest to find enough trees to make logging worthwhile.

Foresters like, ideally, to grow timber trees close together in blocks of the same species, so that all the trees in a block are the same kind and age. The blocks can then be cut when they are old enough. But where this has been tried in the tropics it has ended in failure because there are so many diseases and animals that attack plantations consisting of only a single species. In the natural forest the individual trees of each species are usually spread widely, which makes it harder for disease and plant predators to find a particular species of tree.

Experiments are also being carried out in some areas with what is called line planting. After an area of natural forest is felled the most desirable timber species are planted in lines but with many other species of trees planted in between the lines. This gives the forest the variety it needs to protect the commercial trees against disease and attacks by pests.

△ Rubber tapping is a major economic use of the rainforest.

◁ Palm trees are planted to provide oil.

### Agroforestry

Agroforestry involves the growing of crops and trees together. The reason for the success of agroforestry in tropical countries is that trees provide protection for the soil and shade for crops such as beans. The crops provide an annual income for the farmers and in time the trees can be harvested as well. It is often possible to grow teak trees together with crops, and teak is used for making expensive furniture. Once the trees are cut the cycle begins again with the replanting of trees.

Another group of useful trees is the palms. In the natural rainforest palms grow under the main canopy. Palm trees have very large leaves which help to break the fall of the heavy raindrops of the tropical storms and this helps to prevent soil erosion. Palm trees also improve the soil. Palms such as the Amazonian dende palm produce seeds from which vegetable oil can be made. An unfortunate aspect of growing palm trees in plantations for palm oil, however, is that fruit bats—which are the natural dispersers of the oily seeds—have become pests and this has led to many bats being killed.

Agroforestry may well prove to be a useful way of using some of the rainforest lands which were originally cleared for cattle ranching. If agroforestry is used successfully on these lands it will help to reduce the need to clear more natural forest. At present the pattern is that once rainforest lands are abandoned the settlers move farther into the forest and clear more land. If the use of land that has already been cleared could be improved, that will be good news for the natural forests that are left.

## Making a living

Is it possible to use the natural forest as it is, without converting it to plantations or logging it? If the natural rainforest can provide products that are salable, it makes it more likely that the rainforests can be saved for the future. And natural forests are much richer in wildlife species than plantations of palms and rubber trees. A survey of rainforest in Malaysia covering

90 miles was found to have 76 different species of mammals, but when this was converted to rubber and palm plantations the number of species was reduced to 13.

For more than 100 years the natural Amazonian forests have been exploited for brazil nuts and latex from rubber trees. In Brazil, rubber tapping provides a living for about half a million families, so it is an important use of the forests. The big advantage is that the forest can produce latex and nuts indefinitely. In other words, these uses are sustainable. The forest is not destroyed.

In Brazil the fight by the rubber tappers to prevent the ranchers burning and clearing the forests has been a bloody one. In the 1980s, 1,000 rubber tappers, small farmers, and their lawyers were killed by gunmen hired by ranchers.

▽ The people of Papua New Guinea, and their traditional ways of life, are threatened by the loss of the rainforest.

The Brazilian government is now establishing several reserves (called extractive reserves) where groups of local people are given the rights to harvest natural forest products, such as latex and brazil nuts. It takes about 750 acres of forest to provide one person with an income to support a family. Each rubber tapper has an area of forest and visits the rubber trees once every three days to collect the latex.

## Tribal lands

There is a very real danger that the loss of rainforests and the influx of settlers into rainforest regions will destroy the way of life of the indigenous people and all the knowledge of the forest that goes with it. One of the solutions to this problem is to give indigenous people rights to own the land they have traditionally used.

The South American country of Colombia is a leader in recognizing the land rights of native tribes. The Yakuna Indians, who live in the northwestern part of the Amazon basin, now legally own the lands they live on. The government sees this as the best way of preserving both the rainforests and their culture. They recognize that the Indians, with their knowledge of the forests and with their own laws and beliefs, are the best stewards of the forest and can be relied upon to protect it from illegal settlers provided they are given government support.

## National parks

Another solution being adopted by most rainforest-owning countries is the setting up of national parks. In many of these parks a central core area is set aside to be left in a natural state, with no logging or hunting allowed.

Outside the core, though, are areas in which the indigenous people are allowed to exploit the forest resources to some extent. These areas are called buffer areas, because they act as a protection zone around the core. Such national parks need to be as large as possible, at least 1,000 square miles, to be sure of being large enough to allow the full range of rainforest species to live.

## In Africa

The African rainforests are, with one or two exceptions, less well developed and have fewer species than the rainforests in South America and Southeast Asia.

One of the exceptions is the Korup area. International conservation bodies such as the World Wide Fund for Nature are concentrating their efforts into this Park, where it is hoped to develop ways of conserving rainforests which can be used in other places.

The Park also protects the Korup river basin. At the mouth of the Korup River are mangrove swamps which are the nursery grounds for young fish. The fishing is worth about $15 million a year to local fishermen. If the forests are destroyed then mud will wash into the river and damage the mangrove swamps and the fish nursery.

The Park has been divided into zones. In the center is a core area. Outside the core is another area where people can live and use the forest for collecting plants and hunting wild animals such as the duiker antelope and the cane rat. There has been a big effort to develop employment in the area. Rural crafts, such as rattan weaving, have been encouraged. The long leaves of the rattan climbing palms are woven into baskets and exported to neighboring Nigeria.

The Korup Park shows how important it is to involve local people in finding ways of saving the natural forests from the clearing and hunting that increases as human populations increase. When local people see that they can gain by caring for rainforests, rather than cutting them down, then the forests have a chance of being kept for the future.

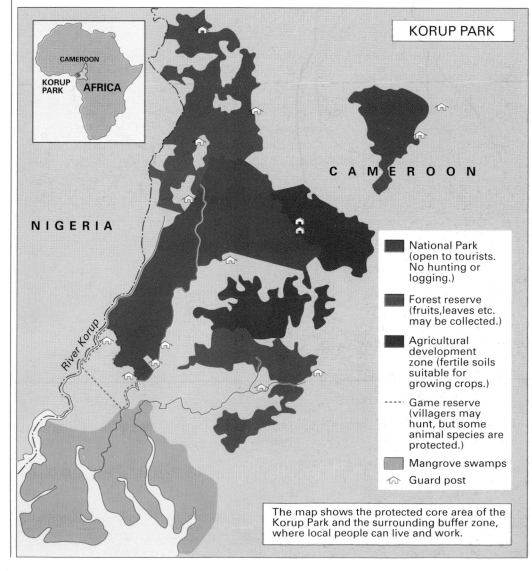

KORUP PARK

CAMEROON

KORUP PARK    AFRICA

CAMEROON

NIGERIA

River Korup

**National Park** (open to tourists. No hunting or logging.)

**Forest reserve** (fruits, leaves etc. may be collected.)

**Agricultural development zone** (fertile soils suitable for growing crops.)

----- **Game reserve** (villagers may hunt, but some animal species are protected.)

**Mangrove swamps**

⌂ **Guard post**

The map shows the protected core area of the Korup Park and the surrounding buffer zone, where local people can live and work.

◁ The Korup Park contains some of the oldest areas of rainforest refugia in Africa (see page 8). The Korup rainforest may be 150 million years old. It has, probably because of its great age, the largest variety of plants and animals in West Africa. Half of the bird species which live in Cameroon are found in the Park.

## In Peru

The Peruvian Government has set up the largest national park in the world to encourage both nature conservation and the preservation of the way of life of native people. Manu National Park is centered around the Manu River, at the head of the Amazon River. The park covers almost 4 million acres and is particularly rich in plant and bird species. It is possibly one of the ice age refugia. So far scientists have found 1,000 species of birds, 13 species of monkeys, 110 species of bats and more than 15,000 species of plants in the park. This area is one of the few in Central and South America large enough to protect the large mammal predators such as the jaguar, and it is one of the few areas in the South American tropics where monkeys and deer are common.

The Peruvian Government is encouraging nature tourism as a way of providing jobs and income for the local people, who number about 400, of whom around 100 are Indians. Nature tourism has the advantage that it does not cause much disturbance to the rainforest.

△ Tourists take to the water in a rainforest park.

△ A picnic in Peru. Tourists are taken on guided tours in national parks. The parks may have clearings with shelters where visitors can camp overnight.

◁ Crafts such as basket weaving allow people to make a living from the rainforests.

# Taking the right steps

We have seen how the tropical rainforest is a vast store of diversity. Only now are we beginning to realize how great this diversity is. The great rush to log and clear rainforests, for whatever reason, means that we are in danger of losing much of that diversity by changing the habitat of many plants and animals.

However, there are solutions to the problem of loss of rainforests. The reckless pace of logging can be slowed if we have the will, and the burning of rainforests to produce cattle pastures in South America does not have to take place.

Those of us who are interested in saving rainforests have, however, some difficult questions to ask and answer. What are our reasons for wanting to save rainforests? Is it because we are worried about the effects on world climate? If so, are we prepared to pay our share toward keeping them and how do we go about deciding how much it is and how we pay that share?

Is our reason for conservation that we want to save the wild plants and animals and the wild forests in which they live? If it is, we should also realize that the rainforests are home to people whose ancestors lived and used the forests for several thousand years. Just what part have they and others such as rubber tappers, who came later but have also learned to use the forests, played in creating the rainforest which we marvel at today? Are we only interested in saving rainforest as wildlife sanctuaries, free from people except for visiting nature lovers? Should we not really be concerned to see that rainforests continue to be the places where the people who have traditionally used them can earn their living, just as we earn our living in our habitat, whether it be on a farm, in a forest, or in a city?

These are important questions. Most of the earth's tropical rainforests are found in Third World countries with the problem of millions of people living in dire poverty. Those of us who live in First World countries are very lucky. We enjoy a comfortable standard of living—good housing, food, health care, and education. It would be a mistake to think that the Yanomami or Yakuna Indians do not also want to improve the way they live, without having to leave the forests that have been their homes for generations. How this can be done while keeping the rainforest intact is a major challenge for the future.